For:

DEAR FRIEND

Compiled by
Suzanne Beilenson

Design by
Lesley Ehlers

Peter Pauper Press, Inc.
White Plains, New York

DEAR FRIEND

Contents

Introduction

Some friends grew up together. Some met in school, or at work. Still others were neighbors by chance. No matter how you made your friends, they are the foundations of your life. They are there for you when you need a shoulder to lean on, and they are the first to help you celebrate. Your friends fill your life with love, loyalty, and laughter. So, if you ever had trouble finding the right words to express how much you care, or if you wanted to help with a little affectionate advice, just turn the page. We have collected a bouquet of quotes about the joys of friendship as well as some friendly wisdom you can share.

S. B.

The Joys of
Friendship

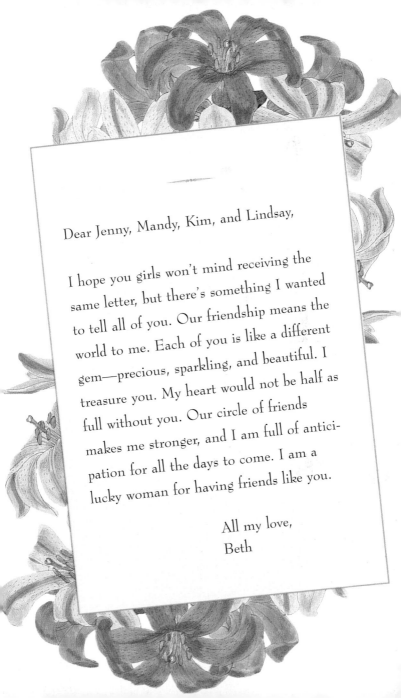

Dear Jenny, Mandy, Kim, and Lindsay,

I hope you girls won't mind receiving the same letter, but there's something I wanted to tell all of you. Our friendship means the world to me. Each of you is like a different gem—precious, sparkling, and beautiful. I treasure you. My heart would not be half as full without you. Our circle of friends makes me stronger, and I am full of antici-pation for all the days to come. I am a lucky woman for having friends like you.

All my love,
Beth

$\mathcal{A}$ friend is one who is here today and here tomorrow.

Anonymous

$\mathcal{T}$he loneliest woman in the world is a woman without a close woman friend.

Toni Morrison

$\mathcal{S}$nowflakes are one of nature's most fragile things, but just look what they can do when they stick together.

Vesta M. Kelly

$\mathcal{T}$he only way to have a friend is to be one.

Ralph Waldo Emerson

One should go invited to a friend in good fortune, and uninvited in misfortune.

Swedish Proverb

Who finds a faithful friend finds a treasure.

Apocrypha

Friendship is like wine, the older the better.

Polish Proverb

You meet your friend, your face brightens—you have struck gold.

Kassia

Friendships, like geraniums, bloom in kitchens.
Love runs up and down a flight of stairs . . .

Blanche H. Gelfant

When friends stop being frank and useful to each
other, the whole world loses some of its radiance.

Anatole Broyard

A true friend is the most precious of all posses-
sions and the one we take least thought about
acquiring.

Duc de La Rochefoucauld

To be rich in friends is to be poor in nothing.

Lilian Whiting

Friendship is almost always the union of a part of one mind with a part of another; people are friends in spots.

George Santayana

Ｉ always felt that the great high privilege, relief and comfort of friendship was that one had to explain nothing.

Katherine Mansfield

True friendship comes when silence between two people is comfortable.

Dave Tyson Gentry

Ｉ can't be your friend and your flatterer too.

Proverb

The friend does not count his friends on his fingers; they are not numerable.

Henry David Thoreau

It is not so much our friends' help that helps us as the confident knowledge that they will help us.

Epicurus

A hedge between keeps friendship green.

Proverb

The more we love our friends, the less we flatter them; it is by excusing nothing that pure love shows itself.

Molière

Never explain. A friend who needs explanation isn't worth keeping.

Erle Stanley Gardner

Your friend will argue with you.

Alexander I. Solzhenitsyn

True friendship is never serene.

Madame de Sévigné

It is better to have one friend of great value than many friends who are good for nothing.

Anacharsis

Good friends are good for your health.

Irwin Sarason

❈

Instead of loving your enemies, treat your friends a little better.

Ed Howe

❈

There can be no friendship where there is no freedom. Friendship loves a free air, and will not be fenced up in straight and narrow enclosures.

William Penn

❈

Shared joys make a friend, not shared sufferings.

Friedrich W. Nietzsche

❈

$\mathscr{A}$ friend in need is a friend indeed.

Proverb

※

$\mathscr{F}$riendship is always a sweet responsibility, never an opportunity.

Kahlil Gibran

※

$\mathscr{I}$t's the friends you can call up at 4am that matter.

Marlene Dietrich

※

$\mathscr{T}$he language of friendship is not words but meanings.

Henry David Thoreau

※

Friendships aren't *fixed* things, aren't set, but rather are forces that change—slow up some-times, even stop, go backward, go underground like streams. They're dodgy, as vertiginous as is all charged, contingent experience we can't control. They are best tended by being tended less. And in a long life we will probably have few of them.

Richard Ford

*The Ups
and Downs of
Success*

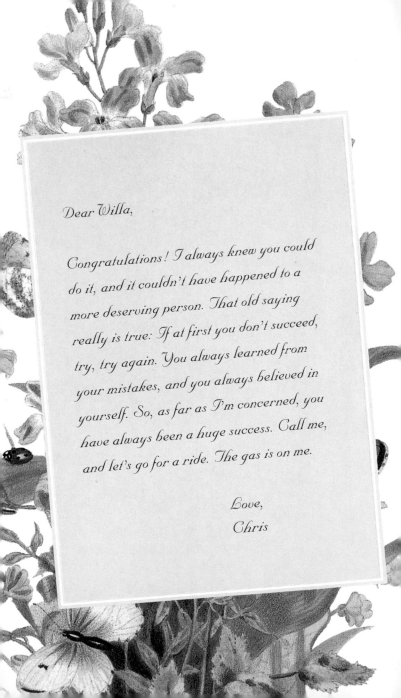

Dear Willa,

Congratulations! I always knew you could do it, and it couldn't have happened to a more deserving person. That old saying really is true: If at first you don't succeed, try, try again. You always learned from your mistakes, and you always believed in yourself. So, as far as I'm concerned, you have always been a huge success. Call me, and let's go for a ride. The gas is on me.

Love,
Chris

Success is not a place at which one arrives but rather . . . the spirit with which one undertakes and continues the journey.

Alex Noble

❋

You always pass failure on the way to success.

Mickey Rooney

❋

You may be disappointed if you fail, but you are doomed if you don't try.

Beverly Sills

❋

As a rule, the game of life is worth playing, but the struggle is the prize.

Dean William Ralph Inge

The virtue lies in the struggle, not the prize.

Richard Monckton Milnes

❋

Great successes never come without risks.

Josephus

❋

Each honest calling, each walk of life, has its own elite, its own aristocracy based upon excellence of performance.

James Bryant Conant

❋

The way to get things done is not to mind who gets the credit of doing them.

Benjamin Jowett

❋

A winner is someone who recognizes his Godgiven talents, works his tail off to develop them into skills, and uses these skills to accomplish his goals.

Larry Bird

The only way to discover the limits of the possible is to go beyond them, to the impossible.

Arthur C. Clarke

What is true of business and politics is gloriously true of the professions, the arts and crafts, the sciences, the sports. That the best picture has not yet been painted; the greatest poem is still unsung; the mightiest novel remains to be written; the divinest music has not been conceived even by Bach.

Lincoln Steffens

Six essential qualities that are the key to success: Sincerity, personal integrity, humility, courtesy, wisdom, charity.

Dr. William Menninger

If you have built castles in the air, your work need not be lost; that is where they should be. Now put the foundations under them.

Henry David Thoreau

I honestly think it is better to be a failure at something you love than to be a success at something you hate.

George Burns

Being champion is all well and good, but you can't eat a crown.

Althea Gibson

Always be smarter than the people who hire you.

Lena Horne

✳

Nothing succeeds like the appearance of success.

Christopher Lascl

✳

What counts is not necessarily the size of the dog in the fight—it's the size of the fight in the dog.

Dwight D. Eisenhower

✳

The greatest accomplishment is not in never falling, but in rising again after you fall.

Vince Lombardi

✳

$\mathcal{I}$ don't know the key to success, but the key to failure is trying to please everybody.

Bill Cosby

※

$\mathcal{S}$uccess is a journey, not a destination.

Ben Sweetland

※

$\mathcal{T}$his is the day of instant genius. Everybody starts at the top, and then has the problem of staying there. Lasting accomplishment, however, is still achieved through a long, slow climb and self-discipline.

Helen Hayes

※

$\mathcal{Y}$ou cannot have the success without the failures.

H. G. "Blondie" Hasler

The trouble with the rat race is that even if you win you're still a rat.

Lily Tomlin

Of course there is no formula for success except, perhaps, an unconditional acceptance of life and what it brings.

Arthur Rubinstein

The Keys to
Happiness

Dear Liza,

When we had lunch last week, you seemed so blue, and for the life of me, I couldn't figure out why. You have a wonderful partner in your life, a beautiful home, and a job which you find really satisfying. You have gotten everything you ever said you wanted in life. But, I guess that's not what matters in the end. If you don't appreciate and enjoy what you have, life isn't going to feel happy. So, stop worrying about all those little things that you think you need, and spend that energy delighting in what's around you right now. Nothing would make me happier than to see you happy.

Love,
Joan

$\mathcal{L}$ife is to be fortified by many friendships. To love and to be loved is the greatest happiness of existence.

Sydney Smith

$\mathcal{T}$he great essentials of happiness are something to do, something to love, and something to hope for.

Alexander Chalmers

$\mathcal{H}$appiness doesn't depend on what we have, but it does depend on how we feel towards what we have. We can be happy with little and miserable with much.

W. D. Hoard

$\mathcal{T}$he grass may look greener on the other side, but it's just as hard to cut.

Little Richard

$\mathcal{O}$f all the means to insure happiness throughout the whole of life, by far the most important is the acquisition of friends.

Epicurus

❖※❖

$\mathcal{W}$e are never so happy nor so unhappy as we imagine.

Duc de La Rochefoucauld

❖※❖

$\mathcal{H}$appiness is the conviction that we are loved ... in spite of ourselves.

Victor Hugo

❖※❖

$\mathcal{H}$appiness is not a state to arrive at, but a manner of traveling.

Margaret Lee Runbeck

❖※❖

*H*appiness is not a matter of events; it depends upon the tides of the mind.

Alice Meynell

*S*ome pursue happiness—others create it.

Anonymous

*H*appiness is not having what you want, but wanting what you have.

Rabbi Hyman Schachtel

*T*here is no happiness; there are only moments of happiness.

Spanish Proverb

There are two things to aim at in life: first to get what you want; and, after that, to enjoy it. Only the wisest of mankind achieve the second.

Logan Pearsall Smith

＊※＊

For the happiest life, days should be rigorously planned, nights left open to chance.

Mignon McLaughlin

＊※＊

Fear less, hope more, eat less, chew more, whine less, breathe more, talk less, say more, hate less, love more and all good things will be yours.

Swedish Proverb

＊※＊

Do not attempt to do a thing unless you are sure of yourself; but do not relinquish it simply because someone else is not sure of you.

Stewart E. White

*H*ave confidence that if you have done a *little* thing well, you can do a *bigger* thing well, too.

Moorfield Storey

*O*ne cannot collect all the beautiful shells on the beach.

Anne Morrow Lindbergh

*W*hen a small child . . . I thought that success spelled happiness. I was wrong. Happiness is like a butterfly which appears and delights us for one brief moment, but soon flits away.

Anna Pavlova

*M*y advice to you is not to inquire why or whither, but just enjoy your ice cream while it's on your plate—that's my philosophy.

Thornton Wilder

While money doesn't bring happiness, if you have enough of the green stuff you can be unhappy in maximum comfort.

Joseph Rosenberger

Happiness is not perfected until it is shared.

Jane Porter

A happy woman is one who has no cares at all; a cheerful woman is one who has cares but doesn't let them get her down.

Beverly Sills

It is only possible to live happily ever after on a day to day basis.

Margaret Bonnano

The trouble with most people is that they're working so hard for a living they don't have time to live.

Helen Leffer

Unlock your heart—that's the true key to happiness.

Nicole Beale

The Lessons
of Life

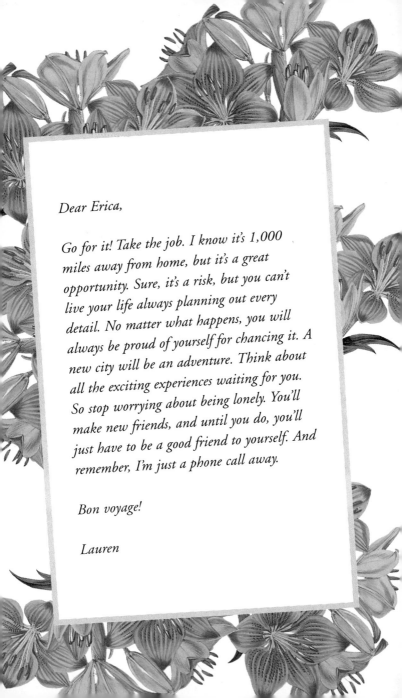

Dear Erica,

Go for it! Take the job. I know it's 1,000 miles away from home, but it's a great opportunity. Sure, it's a risk, but you can't live your life always planning out every detail. No matter what happens, you will always be proud of yourself for chancing it. A new city will be an adventure. Think about all the exciting experiences waiting for you. So stop worrying about being lonely. You'll make new friends, and until you do, you'll just have to be a good friend to yourself. And remember, I'm just a phone call away.

Bon voyage!

Lauren

$\mathcal{L}$aughter is the best medicine.

Proverb

$\mathcal{E}$at, drink, and be merry, for tomorrow we may diet.

Unknown

$\mathcal{W}$e live by our genius for hope; we survive by our talent for dispensing with it.

V. S. Pritchett

$\mathcal{U}$p to a certain point it is good for us to know that there are people in the world who will give us love and unquestioned loyalty to the limit of their ability. I doubt, however, if it is good for us to feel assured of this without the accompanying obligation of having to justify this devotion by our behavior.

Eleanor Roosevelt

The greatest mistake you can make in life is to be continually fearing that you will make one.

Elbert Hubbard

Never put off until tomorrow what you can do today, because if you enjoy it today, you can do it again tomorrow.

Anonymous

It's very hard to live up to an image.

Elvis Presley

Life was meant to be lived and curiosity must be kept alive. One must never, for whatever reason, turn his back on life.

Eleanor Roosevelt

*E*xperience is a good teacher, but she sends in terrific bills.

Minna Antrim

*H*ave a sense of humor about your appearance.

Jerry Seinfeld

*N*ever answer the telephone if you are in the middle of something more important.

C. Northcote Parkinson

A good laugh and a long sleep are the best cures in the doctor's book.

Irish Proverb

It is better to wear out than to rust out.
George Whitefield

Life is either a daring adventure, or nothing.
Helen Keller

To be alive at all involves some risk.
Harold Macmillan

Self-reliance and self-respect are about as
valuable commodities as we can carry in our
pack through life.
Luther Burbank

*M*oney is only money, beans tonight and steak tomorrow. So long as you can look yourself in the eye.

Meridel LeSueur

❋

*W*hat, after all, is a halo? It's only one more thing to keep clean.

Christopher Fry

❋

*T*here are three ingredients in the good life: learning, earning, and yearning.

Christopher Morley

❋

*D*o not take life too seriously—you will never get out of it alive.

Elbert Hubbard

❋

*I*t's true that tomorrow may be better—or worse. But today may not be so bad. You must appreciate the miracle that you're alive right now and forget about how, or if, you're going to live tomorrow.

Rod Steiger

*K*eep breathing.

Sophie Tucker

*T*here is nothing final about a mistake, except its being taken as final.

Phyllis Bottome

*A*ttack power with wisdom.

Jacques Yves Cousteau

$\mathcal{L}$ife is like a sewer. What you get out of it depends on what you put into it.

Tom Lehrer

❊

$\mathcal{L}$ove life for better or worse without conditions.

Arthur Rubinstein

❊

$\mathcal{I}$t costs so much to be a full human being that there are very few who have the enlightenment, or the courage, to pay the price. . . . One has to abandon altogether the search for security, and reach out to the risk of living with both arms. One has to embrace the world like a lover, and yet demand no easy return of love.

Morris L. West

❊

The most wasted of all days is that on which one has not laughed.

Nicolas Chamfort

※

Life can only be understood backwards; but it must be lived forwards.

Søren Kierkegaard

※

There are moments when everything goes as you wish; don't be frightened—it won't last.

Jules Renard

※

Life is an adventure in forgiveness.

Norman Cousins

※

*L*ife is partly what we make it, and partly what it is made by the friends whom we choose.

Chinese Proverb

✦※✦

*E*xperience is as effective a teacher as she is because one does tend to remember her lessons.

Lawrence Block

✦※✦

A person has to be busy to stay alive.

Marian Anderson

✦※✦

*N*o one can make you feel inferior without your consent.

Eleanor Roosevelt

Never invest in anything that eats or needs repairing.

Billy Rose

❋

You have powers you never dreamed of. You can do things you never thought you could do. There are no limitations in what you can do except the limitations of your own mind as to what you cannot do. Don't think you cannot. Think that you can.

Darwin P. Kingsley

❋

Pick battles big enough to matter, small enough to win.

Jonathan Kozol

❋

Be not afraid of going slowly, be afraid only of standing still.

Chinese Proverb

*E*very great mistake has a halfway moment, a split second when it can be recalled and perhaps remedied.

Pearl S. Buck

*T*here is more to life than increasing its speed.

Mahatma Gandhi

*N*ever face facts; if you do you'll never get up in the morning.

Marlo Thomas

*S*elf-pity in its early stages is as snug as a feather mattress. Only when it hardens does it become uncomfortable.

Maya Angelou

$\mathcal{O}$h, my friend, it's not what they take away from you that counts—it's what you do with what you have left.

Hubert Humphrey,
after cancer surgery

$\mathcal{L}$ife is to be lived. If you have to support yourself, you had bloody well better find some way that is going to be interesting. And you don't do that by sitting around wondering about yourself.

Katharine Hepburn

$\mathcal{L}$ife is too short to be small.

Benjamin Disraeli

$\mathcal{T}$oday is the first day of the rest of your life.

Abbie Hoffman

The Qualities of
a Good Friend

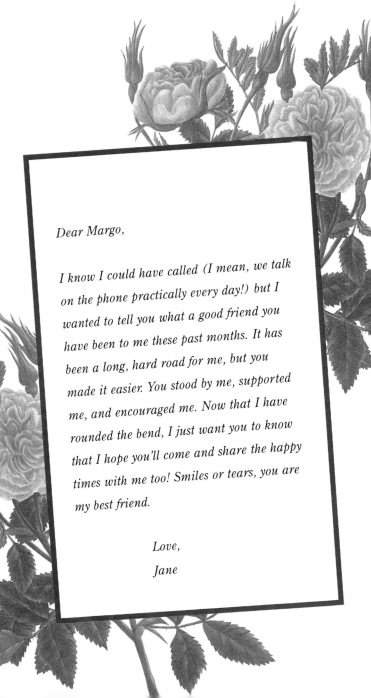

Dear Margo,

I know I could have called (I mean, we talk on the phone practically every day!) but I wanted to tell you what a good friend you have been to me these past months. It has been a long, hard road for me, but you made it easier. You stood by me, supported me, and encouraged me. Now that I have rounded the bend, I just want you to know that I hope you'll come and share the happy times with me too! Smiles or tears, you are my best friend.

Love,
Jane

You can make more friends in two months by becoming interested in other people than you can in two years by trying to get other people interested in you.

Dale Carnegie

❈

The man who treasures his friends is usually solid gold himself.

Marjorie Holmes

❈

However rare true love may be, it is still less so than genuine friendship.

Duc de La Rochefoucauld

❈

Friendship with oneself is all-important, because without it one cannot be friends with anyone else in the world.

Eleanor Roosevelt

Friendship is to be valued for what there is in it, not for what can be gotten out of it.

H. Clay Trumbull

✺

Character is what you are in the dark.

Dwight L. Moody

✺

Have patience with all things, but chiefly have patience with yourself. Do not lose courage in considering your own imperfections, but instantly set about remedying them—every day begin the task anew.

St. Francis de Sales

✺

You can always tell a real friend: when you've made a fool of yourself he doesn't feel you've done a permanent job.

Laurence J. Peter

✺

One needs something to believe in, something for which one can have whole-hearted enthusiasm. One needs to feel that one's life has meaning, that one is needed in this world.

Hannah Senesh

❊

A healthy loyalty is not passive and complacent, but active and critical.

Harold Laski

❊

If you're hammering nails all day and not carrying lumber, then your right arm will get big. If you're carrying lumber, your back will get big. If you're welding, you'll develop other muscles. You develop muscles for whatever you need them. The stronger you get, the easier it is.

Mary Garvin

*Y*ou grow up the day you have the first real laugh—at yourself.

Ethel Barrymore

*L*earn how to refuse favors. This is a great and very useful art.

Dr. Fuller

*M*ake the most of yourself, for that is all there is to you.

Ralph Waldo Emerson

*T*he noblest word in the catalogue of social virtues is "Loyalty."

John Ruskin

It has been my experience that folks who have no vices have very few virtues.

Abraham Lincoln

It is my ambition and desire to so administer the affairs of the government while I remain President that if at the end I have lost every other friend on earth I shall at least have one friend remaining and that one shall be down inside me.

Attributed to Abraham Lincoln

---

*C*haracter consists of what you do on the third and fourth tries.

James A. Michener

---

*C*haracter is perfectly educated will.

Baron Friedrich von Hardenberg

How many cares one loses when one decides not to be something, but to be someone.

Coco Chanel

✳

Have patience with all things, but first of all with yourself.

St. Francis de Sales

✳

In matters of principle, stand like a rock; in matters of taste, swim with the current.

Thomas Jefferson

✳

Loyalty cannot be blueprinted. It cannot be produced on an assembly line. In fact, it cannot be manufactured at all, for its origin is the human heart—the center of self-respect and human dignity. . . .

Maurice R. Franks

✳

$\mathcal{D}$on't forget to love yourself.

Søren Kierkegaard

$\mathcal{F}$riends, though absent, are still present.

Cicero